AGAINST THE GRAIN

The Contemporary Women's Movement in Northern Ireland

Eileen Evason

Attic Press
Dublin

First published in Ireland in 1991 by
Attic Press
44 East Essex Street
Dublin 2

British Library Cataloguing in Publication Data
Evason, Eileen
Against the grain : the contemporary women's movement in Northern Ireland.
1. Northern Ireland. Women. Social conditions
I. Title
305.4209416
ISBN 1-85594-019-1

Cover Design: Luly Mason
Origination: Attic Press
Printing: The Guernsey Press Co Ltd

In compiling this material I have talked to many women and given them the opportunity to correct and amend the discussions of the groups with which they were concerned. Inevitably there is the problem that one can write with more vigour of those things one was directly involved in. I have tried however to reproduce the tone of our conversations and offer apologies for any inaccuracies or other shortcomings. I am grateful therefore to Marilyn Hyndman, Marie-Therese McGivern, Siobhan Malloy, Patricia Morgan, Karen McMinn, Mary Kay Mullan, Mary Clarke Glass, Kate Kelly, Anne Graham, Oonagh Maron, Joyce McCartan, Iris Adair, Maggie Feeley, Joanna McMinn, Stella Mahon, Miriam Titterton, Ellen McVeigh, Karen Mullan and Monica Hynds. Special thanks are due to Lynda Edgerton and Ann Hope who allowed me access to their own files and records and to the Northern Ireland Voluntary Trust for its financial help with this project. I would also wish to remember Madge Davidson who died earlier this year and whose contribution will be sadly missed.

Finally I am grateful to Róisín Conroy and Ailbhe Smyth of Attic Press who have remained supportive through all of the delays and catastrophies that have attended my acquisition, whilst writing this book, of word processing skills.

CONTENTS

FOREWORD

In 1974 I was sitting in my office in Coleraine when a woman called to inquire where the nearest women's group was. I wasn't entirely sure what she was referring to but certainly there was nothing of the kind in the area. We had a number of discussions, talked to other women and the result was the Coleraine Women's Group. Subsequently, a commitment that started out as one evening a week seemed to take over my whole life. I was involved in the early years of the Northern Ireland Women's Rights Movement (NIWRM) and spent many years in Women's Aid.

There was also the Women's Law and Research Group (WLRG) and later Foyle Day Care Association and Triangle Women's Housing Association. Like so many other women I went through years when there seemed to be so much going on and no time to reflect or record. The need for such was evident to me when a few years ago I was asked to give a paper to the Women's Studies Forum at University College Dublin (UCD) on the development of the women's movement in Northern Ireland. The material available seemed limited and my own memory was a jumble of half-forgotten debates and action. In this account I have tried to produce the kind of factual record I would have found helpful then and I hope it will be of use to others.

I have focused on the groups with a specifically feminist orientation that have existed in Northern Ireland and given some attention to community women's groups. In a short book it has not been possible to examine the role played by women in other contexts over the past twenty years. This means I have not considered the role women have played, and continue to play, in the trade unions. Nevertheless, the strength of the women in the Nation Union of Public Employees (NUPE), for example, has been a vital support. At the other end of the spectrum the Northern Ireland Equal Opportunities Commission (NI EOC) has turned into the most dynamic of enforcement agencies, challenging government and employers alike. Much remains to be done and this book is only a start.

1
INTRODUCTION

We need a defiant realism because there is so much to be defied. A realism which enables us to confront difficulty without losing hope, to acknowledge differences between women without bitter personalised and draining divisiveness. We don't have to like each other but we do have to work together - working class, middle class; urban, suburban, rural; heterosexual, lesbian; north and south and east and west; employed and unemployed.

Nell McCafferty 1989

This pamphlet sets out to chart the beginnings and development of feminism and the women's movement in Northern Ireland over the past twenty years. I was persuaded to undertake this exercise for a number of reasons. Firstly, as I think the following pages show, over the past two decades a number of women in Northern Ireland have sought, in the most unpromising of contexts, to clear a space for feminist perspectives. Women have worked in a variety of ways to translate their feminism into practical action, challenging the oldest and most fundamental of oppressions: that based on gender. This in itself seems worth recording.

It may, and indeed has been argued, that Northern Ireland does not have, and never has had, a women's movement. This controversy clearly hinges on the issue of definition. Those seeking a strong network of groups with a united perspective will be disappointed as will anyone assuming that feminism in Northern Ireland must in its theory integrate feminism and nationalism and in its practice form part of the broader struggle against British imperialism. On the other hand if by a women's movement we mean a network of autonomous groups with differences which reflect the diversity of feminist theory itself, but which nevertheless focus on the oppression that women experience because they are women, then such a phenomenon, small and rather ragged round the edges, has existed for some time.

Secondly, charting the evolution of this movement allows us to think more clearly about the issue of diversity. All movements operate in their own special framework and ours has been more appalling than many. The differences that have emerged however, whilst owing much to that context, have also related to broader differences relating to competing strands of feminism. In Northern Ireland we are blessed with radical feminists, socialist feminists, liberal/reformist feminists and there have been recent sightings of metaphysical feminists. We have feminists who are radical or socialist but have yet to be convinced that the reunification of Ireland will significantly advance the cause of women's liberation. We also have feminists who cannot envisage any real progress until the national question has been resolved.Nor, as is sometimes supposed, have developments been confined to Belfast. Women's groups have emerged and disappeared across Northern Ireland in Coleraine, Craigavon, Derry, Omagh, Ballymena and Newry, for example.

For some this diversity may be a reflection of failure - nothing will ever be resolved until our differences are dealt with - preferably by everyone else seeing the error of their ways. For others the differences have been almost an advantage - very little would have survived if all of the women's groups in Northern Ireland had been locked into the issues which traumatised some elements in the movement in the early eighties.

The view on our differences which seems to have gained most ground over the past few years, however, is that they are a fact of life. The real challenge is to find ways of accepting and respecting what divides us whilst at the same time identifying opportunities for cooperation and mutual support.

Thirdly, there are the consequences of the lack of any factual record of what has been done. Issues may be taken up, or campaigns started, without an awareness of past efforts and the information and knowledge that has already been built up. Women with a newly growing interest in feminism in Northern Ireland have nothing to relate to - no context in which they can place themselves. Women become involved in projects but have little access to information on how these developed or why they were necessary in the first place. Beyond this we find ourselves responding to requests for information from journalists, PhD students and so on: information which we've never had the time to pull together.

Fourthly, without a record, confusion and crude analysis persist. Repeatedly over the years I have had a cluster of questions put to me which seem, in themselves, to be based on assumptions which are questionable. A constant question is 'Why have protestant women not been involved/more involved in the women's movement in Northern Ireland?' In my experience, there have, in fact, been many active women from the majority community but they have been involved as women rather than as protestant or unionist women.

Account must, of course, be taken of the obstacles in the way of involvement by protestant working class women which were particularly formidable in the early seventies: the difficulty of challenging the state with which they identified and which was under threat. Thus some protestant women were deterred from taking part in one of the earliest of women's campaigns, the protest against the withdrawal of free milk in schools, on the grounds that anything which smacked of protest or was concerned with rights must by definition be allied to republicanism. This difficulty has, I think, been much reduced. The real issue is not that protestant women have not been involved, they have, but that whereas women from the minority community have sought to link up these two aspects of their lives protestant women have not. Clearly, doctrines of ascendancy and dominance cannot be reconciled with feminism. It remains the case however that many women would for the moment wish to retain the link with Britain and some are not prepared to abandon their sense of identity.

Beyond the assumption that protestant women have stood apart from the whole process there is the view that the development of feminism was the result of the arrival of a number of feminists from England intent on enlightening their sisters in Northern Ireland. This account is deeply insulting to the Northern Irish women involved and overlooks the fact that many of the non-Northern Ireland activists had lived here for some time and had as much to learn as everyone else.

Apart from the geographical origins of the early activists there is also the question of class. 'Why didn't the movement include working class women and address their needs?' one is asked. I think the record shows that it did and continues to do so.

In my experience the unusual thing about the Northern Ireland movement has been that it was, and is, dominated to a greater extent than elsewhere by older women, working class women and women with children. In addition, of course, many 'middle class', in other words university-educated women, have working class backgrounds.

Another question is: 'Why didn't / don't you work with the trade unions and others to raise women's issues and campaign on unemployment, poverty and so on?' To some of us at least this question makes little sense. Over the past decade the real problem has been one of burn-out amongst women trying to maintain their involvement in the women's movement alongside their work in their trade unions, pressure groups and voluntary organisations and at the same time to link up these different forms of action.

Finally, there is the view that whatever gains were made came easily as a result of direct rule from Westminster. The record suggests however that, whilst there was certainly more room to manoeuvre during the latter part of the seventies when we were dealing with a Labour government, nothing was handed to us on a plate.

Clearly therefore there is a need for a basic history but it is not my intention to suggest that life for women in Northern Ireland has been transformed during this period. Much of the old framework remains. Northern Ireland women still travel in their thousands each year to England for abortions. Northern Ireland is still the only region in the United Kingdom without a single state day nursery. Women are hemmed in and oppressed to an obviously greater extent than elsewhere. Nevertheless attitudes have altered to a noticeable degree, rights have been gained,policies have been changed and services that women need have been developed. All of this has been the result of women's efforts. As the following pages show nothing would have happened if women had not acted for themselves.

2
BACKGROUND AND SUMMARY (1970-1990)

In 1970 Northern Ireland was a region of escalating violence and deep deprivation. High unemployment, the worst housing in the United Kingdom and low wages produced startlingly high levels of poverty visited to a disproportionate extent on the minority community (Evason 1976). In 1967 the Northern Ireland Civil Rights Association (NICRA) was formed to challenge the evident injustice which was the legacy of fifty years of unionist rule, later documented in the Cameron report. In its approach NICRA owed much to the American civil rights movement and the civil rights marches in Northern Ireland in 1968 and 1969 were met with similar hostility and violence. The crisis deepened in August 1969 when thirteen people were killed in the Battle of the Bogside in Derry. British troops were sent to Northern Ireland. In 1970 a change of government at Westminster brought a change of policy and attitude. The Falls curfew, internment without trial, Bloody Sunday and the bombing campaign of the provisional IRA (Irish Republican Army) followed. The protestant paramilitary organisations grew in strength and direct rule from Westminster was introduced in 1972. In 1974 protestant paramilitary action brought down the short-lived power sharing Executive and brought Northern Ireland to the edge of collapse. In 1981 the protest against the withdrawal of Special Category Status culminated in the deaths of Bobby Sands and nine other hunger strikers. In 1985 the Anglo-Irish Agreement was signed and there was an upsurge of protest from the majority community. Across the eighties atrocities have continued to be committed by all parties to the conflict.

Against this background it has been the women of Northern Ireland who for decades have taken the bulk of the strain and hardship produced by Northern Ireland's political and economic problems. They have done this despite the added burden of their own oppression. Mary Nelis, a remarkable activist from Derry, has vividly described the lives of the women of Derry as she grew up:

> *The Derry of my childhood was a place of women, strong, wonderful women struggling amid the poverty,*

> *dirt and disease of the overcrowded ghettoes. Housebound, childbound, workbound, their energies diverted into producing children and shirts, the women of Derry were content to leave the politics to the powermen, their souls to the church and their bodies to their husbands.*
>
> *Mary Nelis 1989*

Forty years later in many respects the position had changed little in Derry or across Northern Ireland. Northern Ireland had more unfit housing and poverty than any other UK region and, as Lynda Edgerton (1986) has documented, Northern Ireland remained a deeply oppressive, conservative society with a rigid perception of women's role and duties. On the one side there was the catholic church - fast becoming the most reactionary branch of catholicism in Western Europe - and on the other an equally conservative protestantism with a strong dose of the fundamentalism normally associated with the deep south of the United States of America. The political parties, trade unions and all other significant organisations were heavily male dominated. Women were wives and mothers subordinate to husbands and churches. The churches were united in their opposition to divorce and sex education and catholic women were additionally handicapped with regard to the use of family planning services. Women's responsibility for childcare had been underlined when, at the end of the Second World War, the limited child care facilities that had been made available were closed down - despite strong opposition from working class women in Belfast (E McShane 1984).

The tradition of women working in the textile industry in Northern Ireland had thus not resulted in greater independence for women generally or even an acceptance of their right to work. There is little evidence that the men on the dole 'played a woman's role', women were confined to a narrow sector of poorly paid employment. As late as 1976 the appointment of the first postwoman in Northern Ireland was a matter of much media comment. The applications by three women (alongside ninety-five men) for top jobs in Harland and Woolf was enough to provoke headlines in the local papers (Lynda Edgerton 1986).

Not surprisingly therefore the women's movement in Northern Ireland appeared later than elsewhere. The crisis of the late sixties and early seventies left little energy for consideration of the re-emergence of feminism and the growing women's movements in the United States of America and Western Europe which occurred in the late sixties. As a result there is evidence of only limited and scattered efforts by women in Northern Ireland to link up with these broader trends between 1970 and 1975. From 1975 there was substantial growth however. The level of conflict changed in nature and declined. There was a little more room to think and act, increased contact between the few groups that existed, and growing contact with the women's movements in Britain and Ireland.

In this second phase of development, roughly speaking between 1975 and 1981, as the level of action grew so did divisions and differences. In part these related to the process of women grouping themselves around the different perspectives which exist within feminism as such and in part they related to different perspectives on the appropriate response of feminists to the particular context in which we found ourselves. In the third phase of development, from 1980 on, most of those groups already in existence continued to work on the issues they were particularly concerned with, new groups emerged, and there were various attempts to secure greater unity or at least understanding. Alongside all of this there was a substantial growth in community women's groups. Nevertheless this third phase has been a less positive experience. In part this was a consequence of the divisions but in part it was perhaps inevitable; the intensity and enthusiasm of the seventies could not have been sustained indefinitely. Most importantly, however, there has been the corrosive and demoralising effect of Thatcherism. Enormous effort has gone into defensive rather than positive creative action. Nevertheless the most recent women's conference in Northern Ireland held in 1990 was attended by so many women and generated so much interest that it is clear that there is a stronger basis for the 1990s than might have been expected. The question to be resolved however is whether or not we have the capacity to take advantage of this.

3
EARLY BEGINNINGS (1970-1975)

Introduction

In this first and hesitant phase of development three specifically feminist groups emerged. Two were based in Belfast and the third in Coleraine.

The Lower Ormeau Women's Group (LOWG)

This was probably the first women's group as such in Northern Ireland and it met for less than a year in 1972/73. It contained, however, a number of women who would be active in some of the more lasting efforts that followed. There were approximately ten women in the LOWG which was a general feminist/consciousness raising group. Their interest in feminism was a development out of their involvement in radical and local community politics. In the midst of the massive upheaval of population occurring in Belfast at this time and the growing conflict LOWG produced two issues of a magazine: a venture that ceased when the duplicator 'fell to pieces in someone's front room.' Shortly afterwards the group ceased to meet but some members then became involved in the Queen's University Women's Liberation Group.

Queen's University Women's Liberation Group

This group emerged in 1973. It was a mixed group, as Margaret Ward records:

> *I thought men were as valid a part of the women's movement as women were and it was really the experience of being in the group with men that started making me rethink that.*
>
> *Margaret Ward 1987.*

The Queens group developed contacts with the emerging gay movement of this time. Members attended a conference organised in 1973 by gay and lesbian students at the University in Coleraine. They were active in the efforts which followed to set up a broad movement to link up women's oppression and the oppression of gays and lesbians in what was ambitiously called the Unions for Sexual Freedoms in Ireland. In March 1975 the group was involved in organising the weekend of women's films which led to the formation of the Northern Ireland Women's Rights Movement. The Queen's group was dissolved shortly afterwards. Some of the women from the group joined the NIWRM and later on the Socialist Women's Group.

Coleraine Women's Group (CWG)

Coleraine Women's Group was started in 1974. Initially the group was made up mainly of university women - students, academics and other staff - joined later by women from a nearby housing estate. The intention was to have a discussion/consciousness raising group but alongside this CWG became involved in a number of campaigns. Soon after the group's formation it was learned that the sex discrimination legislation proposed for Britain would not extend to Northern Ireland. Northern Ireland already had equal pay legislation - introduced at the same time as the British legislation in 1970. Like the British legislation this did not become effective until after a transitional period of five years which gave employers ample time to find ways of evading the meagre provisions of the law. The 1970 legislation was however consequent upon EEC membership. No similar compulsion existed with regard to sex discrimination and the government view was that there was no demand amongst women in Northern Ireland for such provision. CWG launched a petition and with the help of other groups 2,000 signatures, plus telegrams of protest, were forwarded to Westminster. An assurance that Northern Ireland would get its own legislation was given when the British Bill went into committee stage. The 1976 Sex Discrimination Order for Northern Ireland followed. Whilst CWG and the other groups involved did not expect much from the new legislation, the campaign was an opportunity to raise consciousness and generate discussion on the position of women in Northern

Ireland generally.

In 1976/77 the Coleraine women worked on a wide range of issues. These included: the absence of abortion legislation in Northern Ireland, the exclusion of Northern Ireland from legislative changes in Britain relating to battered women and rape (the latter being dealt with in 1978 with the Sexual Offences Order for Northern Ireland) and the deficiencies of the arrangements for the payment of maintenance to divorced and separated women. The fact that a number of the members of CWG were single parents also led to the group becoming concerned with the problems arising from Northern Ireland's outdated legislation on divorce and separation.

Northern Ireland's divorce legislation dated from 1937 and, for example, placed no value on the non-financial contribution made by married women through their unpaid work of housecare, childcare and husbandcare. As a result divorced women could actually be evicted from the matrimonial home unless, of course,their name was on the ownership deeds. There was much else that was wrong with the law and a number of women in the group had suffered a good deal as a result. In early 1976 it was announced that Scotland's legislation was to be reformed and brought into line with the earlier reform of English law. Once again, there were no proposals for change in Northern Ireland.

Accordingly CWG issued press statements in protest and appealed for persons in difficulty to send details of their experiences to the group. These, together with a detailed statement of the case for change, were sent to the Northern Ireland Standing Commission on Human Rights to which the matter had by then been referred. In 1977, as a result of growing contact with the Women's Aid groups in Belfast and Derry and the particular concern of the single parents in the group with the problem of woman battering, Coleraine Women's Group became Coleraine Women's Aid. The divorce campaign was taken over by the newly formed Women's Law and Research Group.

4
DEBATES AND DIFFERENCES (1975-1980)

Introduction

As groups developed, and greater contact was made between these early activists, inevitably different perspectives with regard to feminism and the national question emerged. The focal point for these processes was the Northern Ireland Women's Rights Movement (NIWRM). Initially the differences within the NIWRM were the predictable ones between radical feminists, far-left socialist feminists and the varying positions between these extremes. As time went on however the differences within the NIWRM and later between the NIWRM and new groups that emerged related to the traumatic events of this period in Northern Ireland.

Between 1976 and 1981 there was the controversy surrounding the Peace People and, more significantly, the blanket and dirty protests by IRA (Irish Republican Army) and INLA (Irish National Liberation Army) prisoners against the withdrawal of Special Category Status. In 1980 women in Armagh prison joined the 'no wash' protest and three went on hunger strike. These events brought differences which had simmered in the NIWRM since its early days to boiling point. The demand that all women's groups should come out in support of the Armagh women produced bitterness and tension. Many women's groups simply refused to take a position and there was never any prospect of unity on this issue. Some, whilst wishing to give support to the Armagh women, did not wish to give general support to the republican movement and felt they were not being given the space to make this distinction. Some were in favour of Special Category Status on humanitarian grounds and were appalled at the suffering that occurred. At the same time they could not accept the assumption that they had a duty to give support by virtue of their feminism. In consequence some groups plunged into turmoil whilst others worked on and maintained their commitment to what they defined as their priorities.

For some women the major failure of this period was the lack of a united stand on the Armagh women. For others it was the refusal to accept that others had different views and equally pressing work to do in their areas of action. It was a complex, difficult period.

The Northern Ireland Women's Rights Movement (NIWRM)

The NIWRM was set up in 1975. The initiative arose out of a film weekend on the theme of Women in Society at Queen's University, Belfast. A resolution was adopted at this weekend that a campaign be organised to secure the extension of the sex discrimination legislation proposed for Britain to Northern Ireland. Subsequent meetings were attended by representatives from the few groups already active and a number of other women. Many of those who were most closely involved had strong backgrounds in the trade union movement, the civil rights movement, the Communist party and student unions. Very few, if any, of these women had had much contact with the English Women's Liberation Movement.

With hindsight one can see that two things were bound to happen. Firstly, the women most closely involved would make use of the structures and concepts with which they were most familiar in setting up a new body. Thus the NIWRM had a constitution which it has retained and a committee. It also had the aim of acting as an umbrella/coordinating body seeking affiliations and support from the widest possible range of organisations but with a particular focus on trade unions. This objective meant, of course, that membership had to be open to men. Thus the NIWRM did not adopt the approach taken by other movements which emphasised avoiding structures and working on a collective, women-only basis. Secondly, bringing together virtually all of those already active meant that, as the different groups concerned thought out their own positions, differences would emerge which were simply irreconcilable within the framework set up.

These issues took time to develop however and in the meantime during the remainder of 1975 the NIWRM worked on two fronts. Firstly, there was the campaign on sex discrimination. Secondly a number of meetings were held to draw up a Women's Charter for Northern Ireland, a list of demands to form the basis for future campaigns. The charter included demands related to equal opportunities in education, training and work, equal pay for work of equal value, better family planning services, maternity leave and child care facilities. For some it was a reasonable but radical document. For others it did not go nearly far enough. The provision relating to abortion was finally included within a subset of demands under a general heading calling for parity of rights with women in England. Some wanted a clear, specific demand for a woman's right to choose. Others felt this would kill any chance of wide support for the document as a whole. This debate has been seen as 'the reformers versus the revolutionaries'. As, however, almost everyone on both sides supported a woman's right to choose, and indeed this appeared without reference to parity in a later version of the Charter, the debate might also be seen as engaging tacticians versus purists.

The issue of parity has also been an ongoing one. For some this has suggested taking a position in support of the link with Britain. For others this has been seen as a device cheerfully used to hoist loyalist politicians with their own petard. 'If we are British why can we not have the same rights as women in the rest of the UK?' The strategy obviously had to be abandoned when the Thatcherite government started to introduce measures which would be to the detriment of women in Northern Ireland.

In 1976/77 two groups left the NIWRM. The structure of the group was increasingly unacceptable to the radical feminists from the Women's Aid groups. They argued, unsuccessfully, that the NIWRM should abandon its hierarchical structure, scrap the focus on equality in favour of the concept of women's liberation, confine membership to women and reconstitute itself as one group amongst many rather than a coordinating body. After heated debate Women's Aid withdrew from the NIWRM though contact was maintained.

The second group to leave was the Socialist Women's Group (SWG). The SWG members shared some of the concerns of the radical feminists but went much beyond these and wanted a clear acceptance of the necessity of achieving socialism as a precondition for women's liberation. It was also argued that progress towards socialism hinged on the strength of the working class and 'whilst the link with the British capitalist state remains the working class will remain deeply divided'.

(Resolution from SWG to NIWRM AGM 1976). The actual departure of the SWG from the NIWRM was the result of differences over the appropriate response of the women's movement to the Peace People; originally the Peace Women's Movement.

Initially, although disenchantment set in fairly early on, the NIWRM, and other groups, supported the movement. The reasons for doing so were set out in a letter, not published, to Spare Rib. The response of women in both communities to the initiative taken by the Peace People reflected, it was argued, 'their weariness with the pointless violence and with the corruption of the paramilitary organisations'.

The support given by the NIWRM was not, however, without qualification. The NIWRM did not support peace at any price and condemned a recent failure of the Peace People to maintain the original position of opposing state as well as paramilitary violence. There was nevertheless strong support for an effort which appeared, at least at that point, to be drawing women out of their respective ghettoes to meet each other. The statement also asked women in England not to support the Troops Out Movement and condemned the campaign of violence waged by the provisional IRA. The NIWRM argued that the bombing campaign was a major obstacle in the way of uniting a deeply divided working class. They also pointed out that it provided a cover for the British government to introduce more and more repressive legislation and strengthened the hands of protestant paramilitaries. Northern Ireland was not Britain's Vietnam or Mozambique and the withdrawal of British troops would lead simply to conflict between two sets of paramilitary groupings, both of them reactionary and with no interest in women's liberation. The victors were likely to be the protestant paramilitaries who had after all recently brought Northern Ireland to a state of collapse in the three week loyalist 'strike' and pulled down the power-sharing executive. It was a complex argument. The SWG left the NIWRM but what support there was for the Peace People amongst women's groups evaporated fairly quickly anyway.

These debates apart the NIWRM concentrated on campaigns and research, focusing particularly on the needs of working class women. In 1977 the NIWRM developed and campaigned on a detailed policy statement on child care for pre-school children. In the same period public meetings on equal pay were organised and a DHSS (Department of Health and Social Services) office, which refused to allow in babies in prams, was picketed. In 1978/79 attempts were made to raise the issue of discrimination against women within the benefits system, events were organised for International Women's Day and the problem of low pay amongst women in the retail industry was researched and publicised. A funded research project to look at sex stereotyping in education was set up in 1979. There was also participation in a number of broader campaigns plus the work to set up a Women's Centre in Belfast.

From 1979 on however the NIWRM and other groups were under growing pressure to come out in support of the Armagh women. The NIWRM did not take a position on the hunger strike by women prisoners in Armagh though it did condemn strip-searching. On the hunger strike the NIWRM set out its position in a detailed statement issued in 1980:

> *We have condemned the British army on many occasions... We have decided to work for a women's movement independent of political parties and political positions. The refusal to take up positions on these general questions is not because we fear disunity and conflict: we believe that sticking to feminist issues is the best way to achieve feminist ends .... the fact that ... women prisoners are demanding political status does not make it a feminist issue any more than the fact that Cumann na mBan exists makes a united Ireland a feminist aim.*

In 1980 the NIWRM opened a Women's Centre in Belfast and gave support to the campaign in the south for free, comprehensive family planning services. In 1981 the first International Women's Day concert was organised along with a rally in the centre of Belfast - and these have been regular events ever since. Activities in the eighties included the publication of the results of an inquiry into low pay in hairdressing, campaigns to unionise hairdressing apprentices, publication of research dealing with sex discrimination in secondary education, campaigns for better facilities in shops for women with children, research into contract cleaning and the provision of a mobile creche for women's and trade union events. The NIWRM published *The Female Line* in the mid eighties, an important collection of Northern Irish women's writing. In 1986 the NIWRM campaigned against the massive cuts being made in the benefits system and on the issue of cancer screening services. The NIWRM also developed strong international links and hosted visits by representatives of the ANC (African National Congress).

Relations between the NIWRM and some other groups have, however, often been strained. There has been continuing difficulty over the policy of admitting men which has been most evident at the International Women's Day (IWD) concerts. The hierarchical structure of the NIWRM has also caused confusion and efforts to reach agreement have occasionally foundered on the problem of who has the power to make decisions. The way in which the NIWRM relates or, it is argued, does not relate to lesbians and to republican women has also been a source of irritation to some. In 1990, however, the NIWRM did hold its first women-only event and efforts have been made to broaden the committee which runs the centre and to work more collectively.

The Socialist Women's Group (SWG)

The SWG was formed in October 1975. This is how Margaret Ward outlined the origins of the group:

> *I didn't want simply to be a member of the Women's Rights Movement as it wasn't meeting every week and it wasn't engaging all of my interest. I felt there was something else that was missing and I didn't know what it was. But I met other women who felt the same, we still felt we were socialists, although we weren't sure what we were as socialists living in Ireland and the imperialist domination of Ireland was something we were all trying to come to terms with and understand how it affected women. There were also some women active in left groups at the time, who felt really isolated. Very few organisations had any programme for women and if they were interested in the issue, they found it very hard to raise it in their groups. So the Socialist Women's Group was formed'*
> *Margaret Ward 1987.*

In essence therefore members of the SWG sought to link a prior commitment to socialism with their growing feminism and to relate these to the national question. The group consisted of some women who remained for the time being in the NIWRM and others from revolutionary left groups. The objective was to develop a programme on women and to have this integrated into the broader programmes of groups on the far-left. The SWG explicitly recognised the way in which, despite women's participation in anti-imperialist struggles across history, their needs are those most likely to be put on the back burner whilst the struggle for change is waged and to be disregarded when it succeeds.

In terms therefore of its ambitions with regard to theory and strategy the Socialist Women's Group was clearly one of the most sophisticated to emerge in the north.

In 1976 the SWG published its manifesto and shortly afterwards began to produce a bi-monthly paper, *Women's Action*. The paper was sold outside factories and on estates as the group attempted to link up with women in the community as well as to develop contacts with revolutionary groups. The SWG was also active in the Relatives Action Committee, formed in the early months of 1976 by relatives of prisoners to campaign on the issue of political status. Inevitably perhaps, in late 1976 the SWG members left the Northern Ireland Women's Rights Movement. Amongst other things the SWG objected to the support given by the NIWRM to the Peace Movement and the NIWRM's refusal to support the Troops Out Movement.

The separation did not however mark the start of a period of growth and development for the SWG. The attempt to maintain a very tight, complex ideological position which related to three massive sets of ideas was colliding with the objective of reaching working class women. The requirement that all who joined the SWG should accept the manifesto was seen as unrealistic by some:

> *There were two schools of thought, one felt that we should dissolve and form a broad based women's movement that would agitate on issues affecting women and the other felt that the SWG should be maintained and that we should form other socialist women's groups.*
>
> *Margaret Ward 1987*

The outcome of the debate was the decision to dissolve the Socialist Women's Group in May 1977. Some members then set up the Belfast Women's Collective.

Belfast Women's Collective

The Belfast Women's Collective survived for approximately three years and had a considerable impact. Marie Therese McGivern recalls that the group moved through two distinct phases. In the first phase, in 1977/78,

> *as well as tackling issues like women in Armagh and supporting pickets and looking at the whole question of imperialism we began to become more interested in issues which broadly related to health - to childbirth and contraception, to mental health and abortion.*
>
> *in Margaret Ward 1987.*

In essence the collective was trying to work on a broader front than the SWG had done. The resultant tensions led to the departure of some members and contributed to the formation of Women Against Imperialism (see below). After this the collective began a second phase of action focusing particularly on health issues. In 1979 there was a large conference in Belfast on abortion, contraception and childbirth. It was at this conference that steps were taken to establish the Northern Ireland Abortion Campaign and the idea of Unity meetings was developed. Actions that followed included the sale of contraceptives in Dundalk and the organisation of the first Reclaim the Night march in Belfast. The group also continued to publish *Women's Action*.

The Collective went into decline in 1980 however. Some members wanted to work specifically on some of the issues raised by the Collective. Others wanted to move on in terms of their own personal development. There was also a feeling amongst some of the women involved that they were caught between 'a rock and a hard place' - unable to come to any accommodation with Women Against Imperialism on the one side or the Northern Ireland Women's Rights Movement on the other. Some members of the collective remained active in the Women in Media Group and the Northern Ireland Abortion

Campaign in particular.

Women In Media

Women in Media originated in 1978 as a sub-group of Belfast Women's Collective. At this point there were a number of campaigns for better pre-school facilities in Northern Ireland. The group made a short video on the lack of daycare provision for use at conferences and on courses. The group then became involved in running training courses for women's and community groups on the use of video equipment. Shortly afterwards the group produced a pamphlet on abortion which was the starting point for the Northern Ireland Abortion Campaign. In 1981/82 the group published a resource pack for women in Northern Ireland *Picking up the Pieces*, was heavily involved in the production of an issue of *Scarlet Woman* devoted to Northern Ireland and contributed a feminist section to the local anarchist paper. Women in Media dissolved in 1982/83 with the familiar pattern of women moving on to other issues.

The Northern Ireland Abortion Campaign (NIAC)

For much of the seventies abortion was an unmentionable and unmanageable subject in Northern Ireland. Many groups tried to bury the issue lest it bury them. The Ulster Pregnancy Advisory Association worked quietly away assisting the many women who make their way to England each year. The importance therefore of NIAC was that it was the first group to really break the silence which surrounded the issue. NIAC organised the first conference to deal with the subject in 1980. In the same year the group secured substantial media coverage when 600 coat-hangers were sent to the House of Commons. Each had a facsimile of a British Airways ticket attached and a message to MPs which read 'These are the two ways in which Northern Ireland women get abortions'. After this NIAC conducted a general campaign of lobbying and educational work. The group ran out of steam in 1984 but the abortion issue has been kept on the agenda by the Northern Ireland Association for Law Reform on Abortion (NIALRA). The prospects for change appear remote, however, as opposition to reform of the law on abortion is probably the one platform that Northern Ireland's major political parties could stand together on.

Women Against Imperialism (WAI)

This group was formed in 1978 by women previously involved in the Belfast Women's Collective who argued that 'The anti-imperialist struggle takes its most intense form in the resistance of the nationalist areas of Belfast and it is in these areas and through organisations such as the Relatives Action Committee that we should work to raise issues relating to women in the anti-imperialist struggle'.

The group met in premises in West Belfast, produced a paper 'Saor Bhean' and picketed a male-only republican social club. On International Women's Day in 1979, Women against Imperialism organised the first picket outside Armagh prison. Eleven women were arrested at the demonstration - eight of them were members of WAI. Subsequently two members of the group were convicted of disorderly behaviour and opted to go to prison rather than pay their fines. There they joined the 'no wash' protest which had started in February 1980. Though a short-lived group, Women Against Imperialism secured massive attention for the women of Armagh and prompted women within Sinn Fein to organise as women within the party. The group also campaigned against the Payments For Debt Act, an Act which worsened poverty by deducting money at source from benefits, and on the general issue of violence against women. In early 1981 'Women Against Imperialism fell apart under innumerable pressures' (Christina Loughran 1987).

* * *

Whilst some groups were almost totally absorbed with the events in Northern Ireland at this time, it should be emphasised that many others maintained a focus on the issues to which they gave priority.

Craigavon Women's Group

Craigavon was built in the sixties to take the overspill in population from Belfast. Located thirty miles from the city it was a planning disaster: sprawling, lacking any heart or centre, designed for cars rather than people and certainly not designed for those without their own transport. Women in the families who moved there were particularly isolated. They were at home caring for children and cut off from the support afforded by the tight-knit extended family which is a feature of Northern Ireland. Often women accepted their isolation as the price to be paid for a better, safer environment for their children.

The main objective of Craigavon Women's Group therefore was to provide a support group for women in the area. The initiative was taken by two women in 1977. One of the women was from Belfast (with no previous political involvement) and had recently moved to the area with her husband and children. The other was a teacher who had been involved in labour women's politics in England and, through her contact with women returning to education at the local technical college, was aware of the isolation of many women in the area. The group consisted mainly of married women with children and met weekly. It was a women only group organised on a collective basis with an evolving orientation towards socialist feminism.

The group set up an education/discussion programme with speakers on a range of issues. It also developed contacts with the NIWRM, local trades council and the Pre-School Working Party, a forum based in Belfast to campaign for the provision of daycare services for children under five. In 1978 the Craigavon women lent their support to the campaign for divorce reform. The group was also very active in the successful campaign to free Noreen Winchester - a Belfast woman sentenced to seven years imprisonment for the manslaughter of her father who had repeatedly raped and abused her. In addition Craigavon Women's Group assisted with the survey of single parents in Northern Ireland organised by members of the Women's Law and Research Group.

Locally the group successfully opposed a proposal by the local council to withdraw funding from a local mother and toddler group which provided one of the few opportunities in the area for women to meet. With the confidence gained from this venture the group then linked up with two other local groups to seek funding for premises and a worker. The idea was to have a project which would span benefits advice and community education as well as providing a base for the expansion of the work of the women's group. Funds for a salary were secured and, after a series of battles with the local council, premises were obtained from the Northern Ireland Housing Executive.

The Centre opened in 1980 - initially on a part-time basis. It was very much a Women's Advice Centre, accompanying women to court and supporting and assisting battered women in the area, as well as providing a standard welfare rights service. It was a women's 'drop in' centre and the community education programme included a strong element of women's studies.

Over the following years as unemployment rose there was a growing demand from the community for a more extended and developed welfare rights service. As a result the Centre was renamed the Craigavon Independent Advice Centre and, as such, has become one of the most effective centres in Northern Ireland. This development coincided with the dissolution of Craigavon Women's Group in 1983. This was due in part to different perspectives on feminism within the group but at the same time the lives of those involved were changing and there was a feeling that the group had served its purpose. Its influence has continued however. Half of the management committee of the advice centre are women, all of whom have been engaged in campaigning on women's issues and some of whom are members of the original group.

Belfast Women's Aid

Belfast Women's Aid was set up in 1974 to provide a place of safety for women subject to violence from their husbands or partners. For the Women's Aid movement as a whole the term violence covers physical, mental and sexual abuse. Belfast Women's Aid was composed originally of social workers and NSPCC officers with a traditional committee structure and office bearers. Women in the refuge were excluded from the meetings and the problem of woman battering was seen very much as a personal, psychological form of deviant behaviour by individual males.

From 1975, however, there was growing contact with the English and Scottish Women's Aid Federations which supported the development of refuges operating non-hierarchically on a collective basis: run for women by women. This alternative structure was based on a radical feminist analysis of woman battering as a consequence of the position of women in society. It was argued that patriarchal structures gave husbands power over their wives and, at worst, sanctioned violence as a form of control and at best preserved an ambivalence towards violence against married women and a reluctance to challenge the actions of men within their own homes. Research (Dobash 1979) supported by the British Women's Aid movement demolished the original individualistic, psychological explanations and similar data was later produced for Northern Ireland (Evason 1982).

A deep ideological division therefore developed within Belfast Women's Aid which was resolved eventually in favour of the radical feminist perspective. At this point a fire, accidentally started, resulted in Belfast being without a refuge for two years. In 1978, however, the group opened a new refuge. The property was owned by a local housing association and represented a great improvement over the previous accommodation. Grant aid was secured to cover the larger part of running costs. Later the group purchased the house from the association and acquired two more houses. In 1987, in a unique venture, the group opened a house to shelter victims of incest and sexual abuse. Most recently, the original refuge is being redeveloped to incorporate the premises next door.

Coleraine Women's Aid

This group evolved out of Coleraine Women's Group in 1977. To begin with the group provided an advice service plus transport for women and children to refuges in Derry and Belfast. The impracticality of this approach soon became apparent but securing premises to serve as a refuge for the Coleraine area proved difficult. To resolve the problem therefore the group decided to form a housing association which could then obtain premises to be leased to Coleraine Women's Aid. With substantial assistance from other women in the community, Triangle Women's Housing Association was set up in 1978 and the refuge opened in 1979. Whilst the group did get funding for one permanent member of staff from the Health and Social

Services Board for the area it never received anything like the financial assistance required and funding has been a constant problem.

The refuge has survived nevertheless and in 1982 CWA expanded its activities by opening a Women's Centre in Coleraine (see below). Triangle Women's Housing Association has also continued and developed. This is a unique project in as much as Triangle is the only housing association in the UK or Ireland managed completely by women and one of its objectives is to enable women to acquire skills in housing management. Apart from the refuge the Association has provided a number of facilities for mentally handicapped persons (male and female) and accommodation for children coming out of care in Belfast.

Derry Women's Aid

Derry Women's Aid emerged from two distinct strands of action in the town. Notable women such as Cathy Harkin and Brigid Bond, now both tragically deceased, had long been involved in housing campaigns and local trade union and labour politics. Additionally there were a number of women from diverse backgrounds but with a common interest in women's issues. These strands came together as a result of a course in women's studies at Magee College. Those who attended continued to meet afterwards in 1976 as a general feminist discussion / consciousness raising group: Derry Women's Action / Socialist group. The group organised a temporary squat in 1976 to protest at the delay in implementing a long standing proposal to open a refuge for women. Once opened, however, the new facility was in fact a night shelter run on the same lines as the accommodation for homeless men in the city and thus of no relevance to battered women with children. The spectacle of women who needed help walking the streets during the day when the shelter was closed was repugnant. Accordingly members of the group took over a large, empty building in the centre of the town and opened it as a refuge. The building was in poor condition and the group was unprepared for the enormous commitment it had assumed.

On the credit side, however, the group had selected premises owned by the Department of Health and Social Services and the Minister of State responsible did not wish to evict the women and children who had moved into the refuge. The property was therefore leased to the group at a peppercorn rent and assistance with refurbishment and running costs was obtained. Nevertheless the building was inherently unsatisfactory and finance was a constant problem. Between 1977 and 1982 DWA not only coped with these problems but also had a high profile in the broader women's movement, was involved in setting up the Northern Ireland Women's Aid Federation and publicly challenged state and paramilitary violence against women.

After this period membership of the group declined and the refuge encountered major financial problems. In 1985 the refuge was closed. It reopened in 1987 following substantial improvements and there was a fresh start with a new group. Currently there are plans to open a new purpose-built refuge in 1992. Some of the original members of the group are now involved in Derry Women's Centre (see below).

A further development that has continued is Foyle Day Care Association. Founded by members of Derry Women's Aid in the late seventies, the original intention was to demonstrate the need for fulltime daycare facilities for children under five - particularly amongst single parents. The hope - encouraged by members of the then government - was that if a pilot project was successful government would assume responsibility for the provision of the service or at least cover the bulk of the cost. In the event this did not happen. However, the Association has survived and offers the only service of this kind in Northern Ireland. Low cost, full-time daycare is available across the year for children from six months to school age. Priority is given to working women and single parents and the Association manages two centres which are effectively purpose built. The two centres cater for a total of sixty-two children and obviously are meeting only a fraction of the need that exists (Evason 1982). Northern Ireland remains the region with the worst record on daycare services in the United Kingdom (Cohen 1988) with the main option available to women being the growing number of private day nurseries which are completely beyond the means of most.

The work of the Belfast, Coleraine and Derry groups represented the first phase of Women's Aid in Northern Ireland. It was a period of endless work and meetings. By the end of this time however much had been learned and the groups that developed in the eighties - Newry, North Down and Omagh - had a good deal of information and assistance to draw on.

Newry Women's Aid

Newry Women's Aid has been in existence since 1983 when the group opened an advice and support centre for women subject to violence. After many disappointments the group opened a refuge to serve the area in 1990. The refuge can accommodate six families.

North Down Women's Aid

This group was set up after a public meeting in 1982 which was organised by local women with support from the Northern Ireland Women's Aid Federation. North Down opened a part time advice centre in 1983 and, with the help of a housing association, the refuge was opened in 1988. Help with running costs was secured from the Eastern Health and Social Services Board.

Omagh Women's Aid

This group was formed in 1982 again after a public meeting. The group opened an advice centre and, after many setbacks, a refuge in 1987. The refuge is leased from a housing association and some grant aid has been secured from the Western Health Board.

Other Women's Aid Groups

Between 1978 and 1980 Strabane Women's Aid operated a refuge to try to take the strain off the Derry premise. Short of money, lacking in members and with inadequate premises the refuge closed in 1980 though the evidence was that it was clearly needed by women in the area. There have also been attempts to start Women's Aid groups in Ballymena and Antrim.

The Northern Ireland Women's Aid Federation (NIWAF)

The NIWAF has played an important role in the developments described above. The Federation enables groups to work together, promotes research, supports new groups and liaises with the British Federations. The Federation launched the campaign to free Noreen Winchester which united all women's groups in the north and received massive public support. There has also been ongoing contact with groups in the Republic. The possibility of an all-Ireland structure was investigated in the seventies. This foundered because some southern groups included men and the philosophy of a number of these was closer to the social work perspective of the early group in Belfast than to the radical feminism which by then dominated the northern groups.

The NIWAF was established in 1977 by the three original Women's Aid groups: Belfast, Coleraine and Derry. All three had been affiliated to the English federation: an arrangement that made little sense financially or geographically. The English Federation was funded by the English Department of Health and Social Security and was unable to assist with the expenses of groups outside the jurisdiction. A separate structure for Northern Ireland was thus necessary. At first the NIWAF worked with a voluntary coordinator and a small seeding grant from DHSS (Northern Ireland). In 1978 a grant to cover approved expenses (essentially an office, the salary of a fulltime coordinator and travel) was obtained. The office was originally located in Derry and then moved to Belfast. From the start funding of the NIWAF has been a problem. The Northern Ireland funding arrangements are less favourable than those for England and local Women's Aid groups are, not surprisingly, more concerned with fund-raising to ensure their own survival rather than to assist the NIWAF. Nevertheless the expansion of Women's Aid which has occurred is remarkable for so small a region and the NIWAF has played a critical role in this expansion.

More broadly it can be said of Women's Aid that in many respects the experience of the groups epitomises many of the dilemmas facing much of the women's movement today. There is the strain of trying to maintain enthusiasm and radicalism whilst carrying responsibility for complex, time-consuming facilities which are an essential contribution to women's liberation and would clearly not exist without Women's Aid. The politics can get lost as meetings are taken up with endless discussions of finance, staffing and the day-to-day problems of running a refuge. Beyond this there is the difficulty of securing grant aid without abandoning basic principles and becoming just another voluntary social service run on a shoestring. The radicalism of Women's Aid however lies in its analysis of the causes of women battering and despite the years of financial problems adherence to the original aims and principles has been maintained.

The Women's Law and Research Group (WLRG)

This group was based in Belfast and established in 1976 by a number of women, some from existing groups, who felt there was a need for a focus on these two specific areas. Accordingly the objectives of the WLRG were to initiate and support research relating to women's needs in Northern Ireland, to campaign for better legislation and to promote greater awareness of the law as it affected women.

Between 1976 and 1978 the WLRG worked primarily on the divorce campaign. The strategy was to keep the pressure on government over the issue and to counter negative propaganda from some members of the judiciary, the churches (particularly protestant denominations) and others. At the political level the aim was to secure support for change from the unionist parties so that they would not oppose new legislation, even though individual MPs were likely to vote against it, and to secure support from British MPs.

After an intensive lobbying exercise the 1978 Matrimonial Causes Order for Northern Ireland was introduced. The new legislation did three things. Firstly, as well as the grounds for divorce being amended, it was now possible for the courts to give women a fairer deal financially when a marriage ended. Secondly, the Order abolished a number of outdated provisions which had made women in effect the property of their husbands. Thus, for example, up to this point a man could take legal action against anyone harbouring his wife against his wishes. Thirdly the Order broke the logjam, so to speak, and the way was clear to move on to further developments in law relating to marriage and the family.

With regard to research, in this period the WLRG was involved in the groundwork for two projects: a survey of Northern Ireland's single parents and, as an extension of this, an analysis of the extent, nature and causes of woman battering. At this point no information was available for Northern Ireland on these topics though some research had indicated the extent of poverty amongst single parents. Research based in Britain had ignored the problems here.

Between 1978 and 1980 the fieldwork for the research was carried out, with assistance from many other groups across Northern Ireland, and in this period also the WLRG worked, in cooperation with the NIWAF, for the introduction of legislation to give more rights and better protection to battered women. In England and Wales new provisions had been introduced allowing women to seek protection and exclusion orders. However the aim in Northern Ireland was to secure legislation which was superior to English law, as this had turned out to have so many weaknesses as to be virtually worthless. Once again the problem was securing support for change from local MPs but after some delay and difficulty the 1980 Domestic Proceedings Order for Northern Ireland was introduced. This dealt with most of the deficiencies identified in English legislation but did not cover cohabiting women. Over the following four years the WLRG campaigned to get this loophole closed and was also concerned with the implementation of the new legislation. Predictably the courts and police often seemed unable to grasp the principles underlying the 1980 Order and failed to use the powers they now had. This remains a problem as the 1987 NIWAF report, *Police Response to Wife Assault*, indicates though the exclusion of cohabitees from the 1980 provisions was remedied in the 1984 Family Law (Miscellaneous Provisions) Order. This also dealt with aspects of women's rights to the home which the WLRG had been concerned with.

Alongside these efforts, the WLRG was involved in campaigns on abortion, the total inadequacy of the law relating to equal pay, discrimination against women in the administration of benefits for sickness and disability, a test case under the sex discrimination legislation and the failure (later remedied) of the Northern Ireland Equal Opportunities Commission to take a positive, active approach to its role and duties. The results of the research relating to single parents and battered women were also published (Evason 1981 and Evason 1982). The two main pieces of work at this point, however, were concerned with the law on rape and the New Ireland Forum. In 1983, in one of the least useful exercises imaginable, two members of the WLRG and a colleague from Dublin gave evidence to the Forum. The evidence was based on a submission (Clarke and Evason 1983) documenting the law and social policies relating to women in Northern Ireland and the Republic with conclusions and recommendations. The WLRG had no particular views on the utility of the Forum exercise but was exasperated that the future of the island of Ireland could be considered with no reference at all to the rights of the women. Predictably, the Forum ignored the issues raised and the attempt by the WLRG to start a dialogue whereby women in the north and south would compare notes and then campaign together petered out.

A continuing concern of the WLRG has been the law on rape. In 1981 the focus was on the levels of compensation paid to victims. After this the work broadened out to the failure of the law evident in a number of cases at that time. After discussions with the Belfast Rape Crisis Centre's (BRCC) detailed proposals for change were drawn up, the views of Northern Ireland's political parties on these obtained and a survey of knowledge amongst the general public of the law on rape conducted. The results of all of this were published in 1985 (WLRG 1985). After a totally negative response from government the WLRG enlisted the help of a barrister and a solicitor to produce model legislation for Northern Ireland. This was published in 1989 and the WLRG is currently seeking support for its introduction.

The WLRG has also been involved, with little success, in campaigns against the application of regressive British legislation to Northern Ireland. For example, the group opposed the enactment in Northern Ireland of legislation corresponding to the English 1984 Matrimonial and Family Proceedings Act (which started from the assumption that a high proportion of separated and divorced women were idle 'alimony drones'!). It has also consistently criticised the bizarre sentences imposed on occasion by the courts here for crimes of violence against women. In 1988/89 the WLRG was, incooperation with the Well Woman Centre and Belfast Women's Centre, involved in a campaign against an extraordinary proposal by the Eastern Health and Social Services Board to concentrate gynaecology services on the Mater hospital in Belfast. The proposal was totally unacceptable as the Mater hospital is governed by Roman catholic medical ethics. 5,000 signatures were collected and the Board backed down.

Lesbian Groups

As elsewhere lesbian women have been the backbone of many groups and campaigns in Northern Ireland. Lesbian groups as such, however, were slow to develop and until recent years lesbian women have been largely invisible. The reasons for this are fairly obvious: the culture of Northern Ireland is a particularly hostile one and, in such a small parochial society where everybody seems to know everyone else, the lack of anonymity has been a massive incentive to gay women and men, to head for England or stay in the closet.

The earliest recorded lesbian group was 'Sappho'. Based in Belfast, this group lasted for two years from 1974-76 with about a dozen women meeting for informal discussions. In 1977 some members of Sappho and others reformed as 'Lesbians in Belfast'. This group had a much clearer emphasis on feminist politics and took the lead in organising the All Ireland Women's Conference held in Belfast in 1977 (see below). Between 1978-78 a small core of lesbian women were involved in a number of informal consciousness raising groups, some of them mixed, which generally lasted for less than six months. In one case the group closed as interest faded away. In another the group divided on the national question. Overall however it was simply a very fluid situation with women moving on and moving around in a very small part of Belfast and of the women's movement.

Alongside this element a small number of women became involved in 'Carafriend', the advice and befriending service for gay men and lesbians. 'Carafriend' started in Belfast in 1975 as a mainly male organisation. Women started to play a significant role in this service in 1976 and to run a women's night on the Helpline in 1978. This evolved into 'Lesbian Line' which has continued in operation ever since.

5
SURVIVING THATCHERISM (1980-1990)

Introduction

In the eighties some new groups emerged, many of the existing groups kept going and there were various efforts to deal with the divisions that had surfaced. The mid-eighties saw an upsurge of energy around the newspaper, *Women's News* and lesbian women became more visible. Nevertheless, rather than moving forward for much of the time we have been trying to defend the few gains made. Women in Northern Ireland have been at the forefront in the struggle against the ideological onslaught on the welfare state, rising unemployment, growing poverty, the endless cuts in benefits and services and the uncaring, macho, managerialism that now dominates so much of the public sector.

The Belfast Rape Crisis Centre (BRCC)

Rape victims in Northern Ireland face a number of special problems. The preponderance of small, tightly knit communities makes the task of preserving the anonymity of victims extremely difficult and a trial can be a very public ordeal. Offences may be less likely to be reported by women in communities which are suspicious of, and hostile to, the RUC. In addition when women live in an armed patriarchy, (on all sides men have more access to weapons here), there is the greater potential for women to be intimidated into submitting to rape or not reporting its occurrence.

The concept of a Rape Crisis Centre for Belfast developed out of contacts between a former member of the Dublin Rape Crisis Centre and the Women's Centre in Belfast. A number of meetings were held in 1980/81 and the Centre opened on International Women's Day in 1982. At the start a Helpline was operated by volunteers for a few hours a week and the Centre was part of a broader structure: The Northern Ireland Rape Crisis

Association.

As new volunteers were recruited conflicting perspectives on the structure and operation of the Centre emerged. In a re-run of earlier debates some members saw the task as one of setting up a standard voluntary social service with a hierarchical structure. The Belfast Centre would thus be subordinate to the Association. Others wanted the Centre to be autonomous, to develop other Centres which would also be independent and to function as a collective with a strong feminist perspective. In 1983 the BRCC secured a worker under the Action for Community Employment (ACE) scheme (which enables unemployed workers to be recruited and retained for one year only) and the hours of opening of the Centre were extended. In 1984 the differences which had simmered for some time came to a head and the BRCC declared itself independent of the Association which established the Rape and Incest Line shortly afterwards.

By this stage the work of the Belfast Centre was expanding and with better funding the group moved to new premises. The number of workers increased and the Centre was open fulltime. In 1986 BRCC listed its main responsibilities as counselling, accompanying women to court, police stations etc, advising victims and persons working with victims in any way and organising support groups for incest survivors. Additionally the group supports research, encourages the development of other Centres, campaigns for reforms in the law and has an education programme to challenge 'sexist attitudes which contribute to the complacency of rapists'. The group places the act of rape within a broader context where violence against women is an integral part of the social fabric of a male-dominated society. BRCC is also involved in organising the annual Reclaim the Night march in Belfast.

As with so many groups the resources available have always been insufficient and the existence of a parallel and more 'acceptable/respectable' organisation, the Rape and Incest Line, has been a source of difficulty and confusion. BRCC has survived, however, and now has six workers. BRCC is funded by the Belfast City Council and the Department of Health and Social Services though fund-raising from trusts is still necessary. In 1990 the group hopefully laid the basis for a second Centre, in Enniskillen, and in 1991 secured premises which provide an excellent base for future work.

The Northern Ireland Women In Education Group

This group was set up in 1982 to combat sex stereotyping in the schools, curriculum and education system generally. In 1986 the group listed its objectives as: providing a forum for women concerned with the education of girls, acting as a support group for women challenging sexism in their own schools, collecting and producing resource material, promoting research, consciousness raising and publicity to promote equal opportunities for girls and women in Northern Ireland.

In its early years the group produced six editions of a newsletter and ran seminars. It also contributed to in-service training courses for teachers and lobbied for a more active and positive approach by Education Authorities to equal opportunities. In recent years these activities have been scaled down as members of the group moved on or left Belfast. The group has however continued, with its main function now being to monitor the stream of documents being published in connection with the national curriculum.

Women's News

Women's News was launched in 1984 and has been published regularly since: to date forty-seven issues have been produced. *Women's News* is significant as a women's newspaper for the north and as the only such publication in the whole of Ireland. In the mid eighties it also provided a base, attracting new women and new energy, acting as a focal point for the increasingly visible lesbian community in Belfast and fostering growing contact between lesbian and Republican women.

The idea for a newspaper emerged from the Unity meetings (see below). Later, in 1982/83, there were a number of meetings to discuss the form the publication should take: a journal publishing 'learned' articles or an open paper produced by a collective in which articles would be published without censorship or selection if they were written by women. The latter option was chosen and a grant from Belfast City Council was obtained with the aid of their newly appointed women's officer.

The open policy produced two sets of problems. On the one hand articles could be published that had little or nothing to do with feminism. On the other, articles would appear which some women in, for example, the community women's groups, would find difficult to come to terms with: articles on lesbianism being the obvious target. In 1989 *Women's News* changed its policy, describing itself as an Irish feminist magazine and defining the articles welcomed 'as those written from a broad feminist perspective'. Material which is sexist, racist or homophobic will not be printed.

Over the years members of the collective have been involved in a number of other initiatives. In 1984 some members of the collective and women from other groups set up WEBB (Women's Energy Base Belfast). The object was to obtain premises to act as a base from which groups could work together, socialise and escape from the isolation in which many felt they were operating. Despite three years' hard work the group was unable to secure the finance needed. More successful, in 1986, was the idea of a broad planning group, including the NIWRM, to organise additional women-only events for International Women's Day. The attempt to include the NIWRM collapsed but the Joint Planning Group organised the first women-only cabaret in Belfast in 1987 and has arranged an extensive programme of events ever since. The 1987 programme included a series of workshops 'Dealing With Our Differences' which led to greater contact between lesbian and Republican women. One of the most recent efforts arising out of *Women's News* was the attempt to form a women's press (Meadbh). The attempt was short-lived, because of financial and other problems, though the publishing group did produce two books - a collection of cartoons and a set of essays by women on feminism and the women's movement in Ireland.

Derry Women's Groups

Over the past few years there has been a substantial expansion of women's action in Derry. One of the central elements in this has been Derry Women's Centre which was established in 1981. In that year the NIWAF office moved to Belfast and the premises vacated by the NIWAF were taken over by the newly formed Derry Women's Collective to provide a centrally based information and advice service for women. The Centre also served as an administrative base for a number of groups including the Child Poverty Action Group, Foyle Day Care

Association and Derry Women's Aid. The Collective organised talks, seminars, demonstrations and social and cultural events. It soon became clear however that the premises were unsuitable for meetings and other activities and that more space and funding were urgently needed. In 1985 therefore a new structure - WISER (Women's Information, Support, Education and Research) LINKS - was established. Funding from Derry City Council and the Northern Ireland Voluntary Trust was obtained and the Centre moved to new premises with street level access and space for a children's room to complement the other facilities.

As well as the information, advice and referral service the Centre now offers basic education courses for women with assistance from the Women's Studies Branch of the Workers Education Association and local colleges. In 1989 WISER LINKS obtained funding for an outreach programme to support developments for women at community level. In addition the Centre continues to organise a wide range of events each year which include the celebrations for International Women's Day and a programme of events for the annual Feminist Book Fortnight. As elsewhere the fundamental problem facing the Centre is that of inadequate and uncertain funding.

Other groups active over the past three years in Derry have included the Women's Right to Choose group (1988), the Women's Health Collective, which produced a video on cervical cancer, and the Bogside Creche Group which campaigned on the lack of pre-school facilities in that area in 1987/88. In addition the Women's Newsletter Group worked for two years (1987-89) producing *Derry Women's Newssheet*.

Groups currently active include the Strathfoyle Women's Activity Group. This group has been in existence for five years, provides information, runs courses and has organised a number of women's health days. The North West Women's History Group has the objective of encouraging women to get involved in research to write women into the history of the north-west. The Women's Trade Union Group is a coordinating group for women trade unionists in the area and the Magee Women's Group based within the local university campus is an action/discussion group which maintains close links with women's groups in the community. There is also a Women's Health Status Group which collects data on women's health in the north-west. To these many efforts can be added the Women's

Studies Support Group which aims to encourage women's access to education and has organised a number of Women's Education Information Days in community centres and tutor training courses for women's education.

Also of importance has been the Women's Council. This was set up in 1987 by the Women's Centre working with other women and groups to bring women and groups together to exchange information, raise issues and provide mutual support. The Council focused particularly on the need for creche facilities in the new city centre shopping complex and raising women's issues in the local media. In 1990 the Council was renamed the Women's Network and is now oriented towards encouraging and supporting local community women's action.

Amongst the latest developments has been the opening of Derry Well Woman in September 1990 - after three years of planning and fund-raising. The centre offers various screening services, provides information and classes and accommodates a number of self-help groups. In 1990 also a number of women formed the Irish Language Women's Group to encourage interest amongst women in Irish language and culture through the organisation of Irish Language Days for women and social events for women and children. In addition lesbian women in Derry recently set up Lesbian line. Up to this point these women were members of Carafriend and the aim of the new, separate structure is to plan and expand facilities and support for lesbian women in the Derry area. A discussion/support group for bisexual women was also set up in 1990. There has clearly been an energy and enthusiasm in Derry over the past few years which has received insufficient attention from elsewhere.

6
THE QUEST FOR UNITY

In most countries the women's movement is fragmented and characterised by sharp debates and divisions. The fragmentation is in part the outcome of chosen methods of working - the emphasis has been on avoiding hierarchies, which simply duplicate the structures challenged, and working through small autonomous groups. The fragmentation is also a result of different perspectives within feminism and all countries add their own particular preoccupations to this melting pot of diversity. The women in England have struggled with racism and the women in the United States have, incomprehensibly to outsiders, torn themselves apart over the issues of pornography and sado-masochism.

In Northern Ireland we have sometimes seemed oblivious of divisions elsewhere and started from the assumption that our divisions are special and our failure to unite a particular deficiency. As a result there have been frequent attempts to deal with our differences. The 1977 conference organised by the Belfast lesbian women was the first such effort though there were no immediate results from this. Perhaps the most useful initiative in this sphere was the Unity meetings which occurred in Belfast between 1979 and 1983. These were monthly meetings which enabled women in existing groups, or not attached to any group, to share information and work on particular issues such as abortion and rape. The concept of a women's newspaper developed out of the Unity meetings as did the 1983 conference which brought hundreds of women together and provided an opportunity to air the divisions of the preceding years on the national question and the Armagh campaign. Less successful was the 1986 Symposium *Feminism - Our Early Years* where there was a notable failure 'to talk about our divisions in a manner which makes us face them and not deny them' (Ward 1987).

The demise of the Unity meetings shortly after the 1983 conference clearly left a considerable gap in Belfast. To date this has not been dealt with though in Derry there has been much greater progress in recent years. It is evident nevertheless that groups within Belfast and across Northern Ireland do have the capacity to act together on specific issues. In the 1970s this was vividly demonstrated in the Noreen Winchester campaign and in the 1980s there have been numerous examples of groups cooperating on particular campaigns. For example, in 1989 the Women's Centre, Well Woman and the Women's Law and Research Group ran a strong campaign against plans to reorganise obstetric and gynaecology services in Belfast and in 1990 Women's Aid and others worked together to respond to the leniency of a sentence imposed for the manslaughter of a woman by the husband from whom she was separated. However, this strategy is clearly however not enough. In 1990 there was a massive response to a conference organised by the Women's Studies Branch of the Workers Education Association and a clear demand for some mechanism to link existing groups, provide a point of entry for those who want to become involved and act as a forum for an ongoing debate on feminism and women's issues in Northern Ireland.

7
COMMUNITY WOMEN'S ACTION

Introduction

Women have been increasingly visible at the grass roots in Northern Ireland. Many women were forced into more active, public roles as a result of the conflict. It was women who broke the Falls Curfew to take food into the area when it was illegally cordoned off for house-to-house searches by the British army in 1970. Women filled the gap in, for example, the civil rights movement when men were interned. Women were at the forefront of the rent and rates strike and campaign against the Payment For Debt Act which followed. Women married to internees and prisoners had to learn how to deal with officialdom in their day-to-day lives and to become spokespersons and activists at a broader level.

For some this may be seen purely and simply as women finding their strength. The reality has been more complex as such changes need not entail a drastic revision of the role of wives. It may be acceptable for women to take on new responsibilities when men are absent but assumed that things will revert to 'normal' when the men return. As Lynda Edgerton (1986) has noted, husbands may be less enthusiastic when notions of equality and challenging authority in the political arena intrude into the domestic sphere. The pressure on women to 'stand by their men' and to be faithful and supportive, regardless, is also not suggestive of radical change. The actual extent and effects of all of these strains and pressures on women in both communities has still to be researched.

Similar questions are raised, though in a less dramatic sense, by women's involvement in community action over the past twenty years. Here women have won some remarkable victories. In the 1970s women played a significant part in the rapid expansion of tenant and community groups that occurred across Northern Ireland. Women dominated some of the most militant and successful housing campaigns, most notably the campaign in the late 1970s for the demolition of flats and maisonettes in Turf Lodge in West Belfast and the campaign for the demolition of the Divis flats in the 1980s. Women have also been to the forefront in the many campaigns over the past twenty years relating to the high levels of poverty in Northern Ireland. In 1971 one of the very first public actions by women in Belfast, organised by women on the Ormeau Road, was to protest against the withdrawal of school milk by the then Minister of Education - Margaret Thatcher. Women marched to Stormont, addressed the City Council and organised a march to the city hall with two cows at the head of the march. In the 1980s women from working class areas of both communities lobbied MPs at Westminster over the cuts and restructuring of the benefits system under the 1986 legislation.

Again, none of this is to say that women in working class areas in Belfast, Derry and elsewhere have been swept away by militant feminism. Women moving out into the public sphere to argue with officials and politicians certainly represented a major change in post-war Northern Ireland but community women's action has often been firmly grounded in issues which can be seen as the appropriate concerns of women. Often demands have been presented in terms of women taking action as wives and mothers: the needs of children, the family and the community have generally been at the centre, as distinct from the needs of women. Such action has, however, clearly led to many women developing the confidence to start thinking about their own needs as is evident in some of the work of the Women's Centres described below. Moreover some developments in the 1980s, notably the Women's Information Days, have had a major benefit in allowing women to start questioning the divisive myths and stereotypes cultivated by local politicians. Women from East Belfast have had the opportunity to discover that Poleglass (the new estate built to take the over-spill of population from West Belfast) 'is not a paradise for Roman catholics' and women from West Belfast have learned of poverty and poor services in East Belfast.

Despite their recent expansion, the future of community women's groups and Women's Centres is in no way secure. In an obviously sectarian decision the Belfast city council recently withdrew the small assistance it provides to Falls Women's Centre and some councillors questioned the need for Women's Centres in the first place. The decision was revoked when legal action was threatened. Ballybeen women's group have also had problems (see below) and groups from both communities have recently formed the 'Women's Support Network' to resist any further action and campaign for proper funding for all Centres. Another threat now comes from the church. Seen by government as a safe haven for grants the church has a growing involvement in, and control over, community development and training in West Belfast. For the future, evading church control and the distorting effect of the influence of the church on, for example, the content of courses for women, will be a major problem. On top of this there is the problem of political vetting: the withdrawal of financial assistance for the employment of, in the main, temporary staff by the Department of Economic Development from community groups on grounds, not disclosed, of paramilitary involvement. To date no women's group has been affected by this though one of the projects affected, in West Belfast, has been much used for women's events and classes.

The Women's Information Day (WID)

Belfast now has numerous women's community groups: Ligoniel, Ardoyne, Finaghy, Greenway, Horne Drive, the Longstone, lower Oldpark. An important source of support linking the Belfast groups together is the Women's Information Day. The WID developed out of a protest over rent increases in 1980. Women from the Ormeau Road linked up with other women and a civil servant from the Department of Health and Social Services with responsibility for community work and a strong commitment to community women's action. The meetings which are held monthly are attended by women from working class areas across Belfast and by some groups from outside. The meetings address specific topics each month but the main function is to allow women to compare notes and exchange information. WID is also a vital link between community women's groups and groups such as Women's Aid, the Women's Education Project, the Well Woman Centre and so on. The WID has launched campaigns highlighting, for example, the problem of dependence on tranquillisers amongst women, the cost of living in Northern Ireland and the cost of healthy eating.

Women's Centres

There are now a number of Community Women's Centres in Belfast with some development outside, for example, in Coleraine and Derry. The difficulty in such areas however has been the absence of the kinds of initiatives periodically launched by government for Belfast which women's community groups have been able to tap into for funds. In the Belfast area four of the more developed structures with strong identities are the Falls Women's Centre, the Shankill women's group, Ballybeen Women's Centre and the lower Ormeau Road Centre.

Lower Ormeau Women's Information/Drop-In Centre

On the Ormeau Road in 1987 some local women opened a drop-in centre which acts as a base for the provision of a number of community services: debt counselling, homework classes, craft classes, summer schemes for children and help for pensioners in the area. The force behind this is actually one woman, Joyce McCartan. In 1988 funds were raised to purchase the property next door and Mornington Enterprises was established. The property acquired has been renovated, equipped and a sandwich bar and chip shop giving local employment have been opened. Other initiatives planned include a cooperative contract cleaning service to combat the exploitation of women currently employed in this area of work.

Ballybeen Women's Centre

Ballybeen estate is the largest estate in Northern Ireland and is located on the edge of East Belfast in Castlereagh district. In 1983 a local community worker got the Council to agree to premises attached to the community centre being used as a Women's Centre. A worker to develop the Centre was obtained under the ACE scheme and the Centre opened in 1984. Gradually a strong women's group came together, a number of courses - assertiveness training, welfare rights and so on - followed, together with the development of broader links through the WID. In 1985 the women campaigned successfully to get the Council to fund the worker's post on a permanent basis. The women also established a summer scheme for children. The scheme was very successful and was then taken over by the Council - despite the opposition of the women's group. By 1985/86 the Ballybeen women were involved in the protests surrounding the cuts in benefits and were taking the council and statutory agencies to task for the failure to provide adequate services in so large an area.

It has to be remembered that unionist councillors are less accustomed to their constituents attacking government and taking them on. They are also less accustomed to being told about poverty and social need in their areas. In 1987, however, the women carried out a comprehensive survey of the estate revealing a high level of poverty due to low wages and unemployment and a demand for much improved services. The report has had a considerable impact locally and led to Ballybeen being included in the Belfast Action Teams programme which assists areas of special need in Belfast.

This success however was followed by a defeat for the group at the hands of the council which restructured its community services department in such a way that the number of women's posts was cut from two to one and the Centre worker lost her job. She has recently been re-employed for a three year period with funds raised by the women from trusts.

Falls Women's Centre

The first Centre operated by Falls Women's Group opened in 1983. It was a derelict building on the Falls Road leased from the Housing Executive on condition the women put it in order. The women managed to make limited improvements but it was never a comfortable, or, for that matter, structurally sound building. Despite this the Centre did enable women to come together and operate an advice / drop-in centre / creche. Shortly afterwards the Centre was destroyed by a booby trap bomb left in a derelict shop on the ground floor of the building. After much campaigning the DHSS was persuaded to lease another derelict building further down the road to the Falls women who raised £30,000 for its refurbishment. The new Centre opened in 1989. The main services based in the Centre are advice and counselling, classes for women and events and excursions for children. More broadly the Falls women are involved in the

WID, the joint planning group for International Women's Day, the abortion fund (a joint effort with other groups to provide women going to England with financial assistance) and the Women's Support Network. The group also has a strong interest in health issues and links up with NUPE in campaigns against cuts in the health service. To demonstrate the deteriorating state of the service Falls Women's Centre conducted a survey of patients' experiences of health care in 1989 and is also conducting research on the contraceptive drug Depo Provera. Plans for the future include leaflets on the rights of young people and a family planning pack for use, this may be slightly optimistic, in local schools.

Sustaining this level of work is extremely difficult. Currently the Centre depends totally on the ACE scheme for workers salaries. As workers cannot normally be retained for more than one year under this scheme the Falls women, like all other groups dependent for staffing on ACE, face the problem of constant staff changes. In addition, the Falls women were, as noted above, the subject of a recent attempt by Belfast City Council to withdraw the small amount of financial assistance it currently provides to the Centre.

Shankill Women's Centre

The Lower Shankill Women's Group was formed in 1987. Premises were obtained in 1988 and money raised to refurbish the premises which opened in January 1990. Help with running costs and the salary for one worker has been obtained for a three-year period. It operates as a drop-in/advice centre, runs classes for women and has a sandwich, coffee bar. The Centre is involved in the Women's Support Network and WID.

Coleraine Women's Centre

This was established by Coleraine Women's Aid in 1982 when the group leased a building in the Centre of the town. The ground floor was turned into a second-hand clothes shop to generate income for the project as a whole. The first floor housed an advice and information service with a craft and resource centre on the second floor. The Centre now has a large education programme for women and provides courses ranging from assertiveness training to computer skills. The Coleraine women receive a small grant from the local council but, once again, rely heavily on ACE workers and grants from trusts.

8
SUPPORTING STRUCTURES

Stereotypes of working class women tackling the issues at the grass roots whilst educated feminists pursue separate, unconnected interests make little sense anywhere and are particularly unhelpful in Northern Ireland. Three organisations - the Women's Studies Branch of the Worker's Education Association, the Women's Education Project and the Belfast Well Woman Centre have been specifically concerned with acting as a resource for community women's groups and linking these to feminist groups.

The WEA Women's Studies Branch

This has a major role across Northern Ireland. The basic concept is that of using education to empower women, encouraging 'those who have not experienced formal education since school to ... use their own skills and personal resources to fight for control over their own lives, environment, work, creativity, minds and bodies' (Annual Report 1990). In 1989/90 the Branch organised forty day schools and workshops across Northern Ireland and sixty courses of between six and ten weeks duration. Assertiveness training and courses relating to health dominate what is requested and offered. The number of courses provided doubled between 1988/99 and 1989/90 and the Branch recently organised one of the largest and most successful women's conferences to date in Northern Ireland. The Branch is currently engaged in a research project on women's studies in Northern Ireland.

The Well Woman Centre

The Well Woman Centre has recently closed due to inadequate funding. It was, however, an important resource for women in Belfast. This facility evolved out of discussions between a number of women in statutory and voluntary agencies, notably the Family Planning Association. The Centre opened in 1986 when a fulltime worker was employed and provided an advice and information service (particularly necessary in Northern Ireland), compiled information packs on a range of subjects and acted as a link between women and the large number of self help and support groups which exist.

One of the most important functions of the Centre was to act as a resource for information and classes for community women's groups. In addition the Centre was also involved in various campaigns, one of the most recent being against the proposals by the Eastern Health and Social Services Board to reorganise obstetric and gynaecology services in Belfast.

The Women's Education Project (WEP)

This project was set up in 1983. The main aims of the WEP are to provide support and information to local women's groups; to develop innovative courses for women in local areas; to provide training and to promote awareness of the educational needs of women. In 1988/89 the WEP worked with twenty-two different groups mainly in Belfast. The WEP has also been involved in research on women and employment. Dependent, in the main, on charitable trusts for funding, the WEP has often appeared on the verge of closure, once again, and has never enjoyed the resources needed to expand and develop fully.

9
CONCLUSION

For feminists in Northern Ireland the past twenty years have been in turn invigorating, exasperating and demoralising. The context has been one of deprivation and conflict exacerbated by the policies of one of the most reactionary governments in Western Europe. The gains have been meagre by comparison with what we wanted but seem more substantial when set against where we started from. We have guilt-tripped ourselves with fears of cooption and at one point or another just about everyone has claimed to be the real outcasts or outsiders.

Sooner or later however the record has to be allowed to speak for itself and we have to move on. One of the most remarkable aspects of the 1990 conference in Belfast was that the conference was declared closed by the organisers but no one wanted to go home. Many women in Northern Ireland clearly want there to be a women's movement and are looking for something. Why are they looking when there seem to be so many groups and centres working away? The level of activity is, and has long been, remarkable when compared with any other area with a similarly small population. Perhaps the answer is that, as the past decade has worn on, the movement has come to resemble a wheel - with spokes and a rim but no centre. The result is a growing number of semi-detached feminists, the possibility that existing groups will develop a kind of ideological anaemia and that, in time, the answers to the question, 'Why do we need Women's Centres anyway?' will have been forgotten.

For the 1990s we need a core to revitalize feminist debate and politics in Northern Ireland. We need it to support what exists, to act as a magnet for new women, to promote cooperation and to challenge more effectively the deeply anti-women policies that have been part and parcel of the crude economic and social theories that made up Thatcherism. Above all, surely by now we have the maturity to clear a space where all women, Republican and Unionist, protestant and catholic, lesbian and heterosexual, can feel comfortable and relate to each other on a basis of mutual respect. The choice between growth or stagnation is ours.

REFERENCES

C Clarke and E Evason, *Women and Social Policy*, Women's Law and Research Group, 1983.
B Cohen, 'Caring For Children', *Report For The European Commission's Child Care Network*, Commission Of The European Communities, 1988.
R and R Dobash, *Violence Against Wives*, Open Books Publishing Ltd, 1979.
L Edgerton, *Examination of the role of Northern Irish Women in their domestic, social and political life*, BA Dissertation Queen's Universtiy, Belfast, 1977.
L Edgerton, 'Public Protest, Domestic Acquiescence: Women in Northern Ireland', in R Ridd and H Callaway, *Caught Up In Conflict: Women's Responses To Political Strife*, Macmillan 1986.
E Evason, *Poverty: The Facts in Northern Ireland*, Child Poverty Action Group, 1976.
E Evason, *Just Me and The Kids: A study of single parent families in Northern Ireland* Northern Ireland Equal Opportunities Commission, 1980.
E Evason, *Hidden Violence: a study of battered women in Northern Ireland*, Farset Cooperative Press, 1982.
E Evason, *Victims On Trial: the law on rape in Northern Ireland*, Women's Law and Research Group, 1984.
E Evason, *Who Needs Day Care?'*, Northern Ireland Equal Opportunities Commission, 1982.
C Loughran, 'Writing Our Own History', in *Trouble and Strife*, 1987.
N McCafferty 'Times Are Bad' in *Fortnight*, March 1989.
E McShane 'Day Nursery Provision 1942-1945', PhD Thesis, Queen's University, Belfast, 1984.
P Montgomery and V Bell, *Police Response To Wife Assault* Northern Ireland Women's Aid Federation, 1985.
M Nelis, 'Real Change Still Beckons' in *Unfinished Revolution: Essays on the Irish Women's Movement*, Meadbh Publishing, Belfast, 1989.
M Ward. *A Difficult Dangerous Honesty: ten years of feminism in Northern Ireland,* 1987.

NAMES AND ADDRESSES OF GROUPS

Ballybeen Women's Centre 34 Ballybeen Square, Dundonald. Tel (0232) 481632.

Belfast Women's Aid Tel (0232) 662348.

Child Poverty Action Group c/o 9 Clarendon Street, Derry. Tel (0504) 262433.

Coleraine Women's Aid Tel (0265) 823195.

Coleraine Women's Centre 3 Abbey Street, Coleraine. Tel (0265) 56573.

Derry Women's Aid Tel (0504) 263174.

Derry Women's Centre 7 London Street, Derry. Tel (0504) 256672.

NI Equal Opportunities Commission (NI EOC) Chamber of Commerce House, 22 Great Victoria Street, Belfast BT2 2BA. Tel (084) 242752.

Falls Women's Centre 149 Mulholland Terrace, Falls Road, Belfast. Tel (084) 327672.

Foyle Day Care Association 1 Kennedy Place, Derry. Tel (0504) 360313.

Lesbian Line Belfast Tel (0232) 238668.
Derry Tel (0504) 263120.

Lower Ormeau Women's Information/Drop-In Centre 115 Ormeau Road, Belfast. Tel (084) 246378.

National Union of Public Employees (NUPE) 523 Antrim Road, Belfast BT15 6BS. Tel (084) 370684/370971.

Newry Women's Aid Tel (0693) 67174.

North Down Women's Aid Tel (0247) 463608/271555.

Omagh Women's Aid Tel (0662) 245998.

Shankill Women's Centre 79 Shankill Road, Belfast. Tel (084) 240642.

The Northern Ireland Women's Rights Movement (NIWRM) 19 North Street Arcade, Belfast. Tel (084) 231676.

The Women's Education Project (WEP) 129 University Street, Belfast BT7 1HP. Tel (084) 230212.

The Northern Ireland Women In Education Group 12 Rossory Church Road, Enniskillen. Tel (0365) 322961.

The Belfast Rape Crisis Centre (BRCC) 41 Waring Street, Belfast. Tel (084) 249696.

The Women's Law and Research Group (WLRG) c/o 26 Mount Merrion Avuneu, Belfast BT6. Tel (084) 646959.

The Northern Ireland Women's Aid Federation (NIWAF) 129 University Street, Belfast BT7 1HP. Tel (084) 249041.

Women's News 185 Donegall Street, Belfast. Tel (084) 322823.

Workers Education Association (WEA) 1 Fitzwilliam Street, Belfast BT7. Tel (084) 329718.

See also Annual *Irish Women's Guidebook and Diary* (Attic Press, Dublin.

INDEX